UNDERWATER

Jill Michelle

Riot in Your Throat
publishing fierce, feminist poetry

Sebacher, Jill Michelle
1st edition.
ISBN: 979-8-9889898-7-5

Cover Photo: Klara Kulikova (unsplash.com)
Cover Design: Kirsten Birst
Book Design: Shanna Compton
Author Photo: Megan Markham

Riot in Your Throat
Arlington, VA
www.riotinyourthroat.com

For younger me, who didn't think she could survive any of this

CONTENTS

ON OUR WAY HOME

We speed down the expressway in funeral-thick silence
miles increasing between us

and the hospital, its doctors and nurses
our son, his too tiny body.

Lost in a one-way argument with a god
I can't quite believe in anymore

flinging how-could-you, how-could-you-nots
at the windshield's low-slung clouds

I don't hear my husband ask at first
Where would you like to go?

and when it registers, picture the baby
things, waiting on our dresser at home

that rubber ducky hat I couldn't resist
the stack of bunny onesies, Christmas presents.

Anywhere but there, I think but ask instead
How about the Starbucks drive-thru by work?

And that is how I end up a grenade
at the intersection of MetroWest and Kirkman

biting my pin of a tongue
while Neil slides into the straight lane

instead of the more efficient left-turn one.
We toddle past the corner BP, take a left

at the tire shop, another left onto a feeder street
where I see what I wouldn't have

if we'd gone my way—
Meaghan, the Comp. II student from Valencia

the one who'd answered the icebreaker question
one thing she'd do on her last day on Earth

Kiss my son's ultrasound picture
tell him, I'll see him soon.

There in the Starbucks window
where I didn't know she worked

was the only woman I knew who'd lost her baby
after twenty weeks

who knew without a word when we walked inside
wrapped me in her arms on sight

and while it was far from the miracle we wanted
it was the one we got.

THIS IS THE FLOOR WHERE NO BABIES ARE SAVED

The first time
you're wheeled up
to the 8th floor of Winnie Palmer
you don't know—
the shock
has not worn off.
The tile shines
hypnotizes
hotel-like.
Then the chair is parked
at the nurse's station
a check-in desk
to the resort
no one wanted.

The first time
you swaddle your hope
hold it close
pray so hard it hurts
for the doctors to be wrong
for your son to hang on
for just a few more weeks
enough time
to make the tiny set of lungs
he needs.

The first time
you don't know
a baby at twenty-one weeks
is beautiful
the size of your hand.

The first time
you don't know
as you're wheeled back out
that a scrap of your soul will stay
packed away for a year
in a closet full of shoe boxes—
row upon row
of unimaginable loss
and too small footprints.

The second time
you know.

AFTERMATH

In February 2007, after the water broke and I lost a son at 21 weeks, my father took me to brunch. Sitting across the Perkins booth, he reached for my tissue-free hand as I cried over a plate of chocolate chip pancakes instead of eating them. In February of 2008, after a second baby died the same way, I took Dad to lunch, sat across the TooJay's table—view of Health Central, where I'd lost a daughter yesterday, where I'd lose him in 2012, over his left shoulder. We held hands next to his uneaten Reuben as he sobbed, caught in the 40-year-old memory of arriving at his first Navy ship only to be flown home at the news of his mother's death.

Quiz on this section:

a. Pinpoint the day between February 11th, 2007 and February 22nd, 2008 when the Alzheimer's plaques overran the narrator's dad's brain.
b. How did the narrator feel handing her babies back over to nurses?
c. How did the narrator feel handing her dad over to the nursing home?
d. Draw a diagram of your heart. Color in its shadows. Label them with the middle names of your dead.

MOURNING SONG

Thief of time, closer of eyes, Alzheimer's
steals your life at sixty-seven—in a hail
of neuron misfires, you forget how to breathe.

I sit here silently, disbelieving your departure.
At the funeral home, the mahogany box of
ashes mocks the living, along with a blown-up

photo I've never seen before. I'm no more your
daughter, or anyone's—twisted disease making
mothers of your young, growing us up as it cuts

you down. All morning your image haunts the
patio where I cobble last words under clouds of
cigarette smoke, wrestle your ghost as he heads

to sea. One last call, and I'm adrift, string-cut
puppet, mouth unhinged in painter's scream
weightless without parental gravity. I want

you back, but the stars have swallowed the
light from your eyes and the ocean, your body.
A shiny new pain sinks me like an anchor.

IN THE LAST YEAR OF OUR MARRIAGE

When El Niño ended
and the rains ceased
our cypress dome—
usually flooded
under feet of water—
held only puddles.
We walked
the siphoned ground
astonished.
Where had it all gone?
Arriving at the lowest spot
we saw in a murky oval
no longer than a yardstick
and barely an inch deep
a pair of mudfish
miraculously alive
half out-of-water
thrashing
from side to side
holding on
to a world
already lost.

TIRED OF FIGHTING

Love, I cannot keep you—orders
Obeyed, and still you are born too still
Six weeks before the doctors will even
Try to save you, so now you live only in

Cruelest dreams—Moses basket in the nurse's
Arms, delivering its promised miracle.
Under the tiny train pajamas, your lungs fill.
Sleepy eyes open. Soft breaths sing in my
Ears, restart my heart—until I wake again.

WAITING ROOM BLUES

Stuck here in another doctor's office with its white-
washed walls, tiled floors, generic décor, pastel-
painted triptychs, slanted pink lines to stare at, instead

of that wall calendar, announcing another February and
casting fourteen years off as fast as that last cotton gown
slid down to a blue puddle on the hospital floor.

Remind yourself: this is just the allergist, dermatologist,
orthopedist—no OB-GYN anymore, no high-risk specialist.
You aren't pregnant with anything but grief. It swells

your belly like a phantom limb. Baby bump grown back
you listen for the ultrasound, the train back on its track.

THE GENDER REVEAL: A QUIZ

We went to the ultrasound appointment:
    a. at 21 weeks
    b. with our 10-year-old
    c. to find out the baby's sex
    d. spotting but hoping for the best

After the technician pressed the transducer down:
    a. my body jolted without permission
    b. I bit my tongue rather than scream
    c. my kid's Big Sister shirt blurred
    d. the technician fled the scene

When the chartless doctor came in:
    a. he told us to expect a call from my OB-GYN
    b. the technician wouldn't meet my eyes
    c. my husband, a bottled soda, fizzed and popped with the god-damn-its
       kept inside
    d. my daughter's hand was a warm anchor on my hip
    e. I knew we'd leave, knowing nothing more than when we walked in

PARENTING LESSONS

Growing up, I hated dolls
those little porcelain frauds

their expressions forever fixed
in pout or pucker

some serene smile
a real baby seldom makes.

Rivulets of the green sugar drink
you pour into the bottle

dribble down pinked cheeks
drip out of plastic bottoms

ruining the few diapers
that came in the kit—

never enough, I thought then
but I've since learned

that having packs of diapers
and not needing them

is worse.

EACH TIME I PULL INTO MOM'S PARKING SPOT

it's 1997, and there's Gram, alive, next to me in the passenger seat after an evening dash to Food Lion for baby things, the bananas she would mash later, fingers still deft at 89, running along the pale spines for strings, telling me how *careful one has to be feeding babies.* I reach over the armrest into the backseat, grab the grocery bag, a pack of diapers, only to drop them at the wail from Gram, face in hands, caught again, stuck in Alzheimer's web, a 1930s string of memories that only she can see. *Michael, Michael,* she repeats a name I've never heard her say, syllables laced with a brand of pain I couldn't place until a decade later when the pink-capped nurses took my son's body away.

NOT AGAIN

In this poem
your ex stops
when you say no
so you never sit
in this therapist's office
some twenty years later
asking Brittany
how and if to mention
to a second man
full of good intentions
full of honor
who would stop
if you said no
to sex
but doesn't stop
when you slingshot
the word
no
a stone
between breathless giggles
under the assault
of his tickling fingers.
He thinks the laughter
means you're happy
thinks you're playing
the same game
doesn't understand
when you say
no
over and over

that you mean it
the more it is ignored
that you've left
the room
the year
your body
again
because apparently
your body isn't yours
just something you drag
between men
some
thing
you're powerless
to protect
again
and it doesn't matter
that it's his hands
that you're fully dressed—
it's you
being touched
how
where
when
you don't want to be
again—
and it doesn't matter
that the last thing
you want
on some random Tuesday night
is to be back
on that other floor

in 1991
again
his continued press
against you
against your words
powerless as pebbles
in a girl's hands
thrown
over and over
against this Goliath
that never falls
just tightens his grip
on your wrists
until he's done
and all of this
the new one shouldn't
have to deal with
you say to the therapist
for picking you
the fruit that looked fine
on the outside
but with this pit of stone
this bruised core
where the one who raped you
can't reach anymore
because in this poem
he stops
when you say no.

WHY, LIKE THE TIDE, HE COULD NOT STOP

The curves of my shoreline
bore his previous prints
so he assumed land rights
planted blooms across my wrists
violet as the moon-dark miles
of the Chesapeake
where the bridge lights
are swallowed like a *no*
by the unforgiving bay—
there, he built
his gaslit tunnels
felt safe.

TRIPTYCH TO WRECK DIVING

I put on / the body-armor of black rubber /
the absurd flippers / the grave and awkward mask.

—Adrienne Rich

here's	a poem	to stitch
the past's	brutal	tides to
bruised	present	butterfly
girl	glue-stuck	cocoons
herself	on bedrest	the future
a woman	an island	bone-throated
hope-spun	unreachable	but glimmering

BELIEVING EVERY WORD THEY SAID WAS TRUE

Four weeks after the worst happened, I'm in stirrups, confined again,
Obstetrician telling us it was *lightning strike bad luck. Try again.*
October finds me peeing on sticks. Squirrelling away my leftover
Little acorns of dread, I smile, pretend our child can't die again.

Fall lifts with its morning sickness. We watch the belly grow
Out of clothes, tell our ten-year-old, pray it will go right again.
Repeating the loss, an unspoken thought until that damned spot

Luckless dot of red at December's end. Then the doctors try again
Order their tests, their needle-sticks, January bedrest, twice-weekly
Visits. Stirrup-splayed, a butterfly pinned, I can't stop crying again.
Everything ends in February—again. No birth certificates are given.

HAVE TO HAVE POISON SKIN

Sofa, table, carpet, ceiling—the
Things he's pinned you between.
A tacked butterfly, the mind, stuck in
Your barbed cage of a body.

Attacked again in sleep where your
Words fall, useless as clipped wings
And awake, one wayward touch traps
You back between sofa, table, carpet, ceiling.

THINGS I CANNOT SAY BACK TO THE THERAPIST AND BELIEVE

My body is mine.
It belongs
to me.

PLANNING MY ESCAPE

Self-defense class starts, and we Girl Scouts, a pack of preteens, are taught to
  walk with
Purpose, better yet in pairs, better still with keys laced between fisted fingers.
  The
Instructor, covered in black pads, reminds us our job is to survive, not be
  nice, as he
Demonstrates how we should follow through on our punches, aim for his
  brown
Eyes; unless he tries to grab us from behind, then we lift our knees to sashed
  chests
Rear back, before leveling our heels at his kneecaps. We practice, and he
  warns
What not to wear—fabrics that constrict, short skirts, tight bodices, hair in
  ponytails too
Easily grabbed. He tells us to ignore our first instinct, taught on TV, to aim
  for his
Balls where the rapist will expect attack. Instead use your weight, go slack,
  then hit hard
Somewhere he's unprepared, like I will be when it's my lover assaulting me.

HOW TO GET THE GUY BETWEEN YOUR LEGS TO SAY
YOU'RE RARE AND INTERESTING

lose one child / listen to the doctors / try again in eight weeks / listen to the doctors / at the right time of month / listen to the doctors / track it on a calendar / listen to the doctors / make sex no fun / listen to the doctors / find you're pregnant in fall / listen the doctors / see the high-risk once a month / listen to the doctors / be a broken well / listen to the doctors / *lift nothing over five pounds* / listen to the doctors / your rope is split / listen to the doctors / no laundry baskets / listen to the doctors / no confused daughter / listen to the doctors / choke down these horse pills / listen to the doctors / drink OJ like water / listen to the doctors / make it to twelve weeks / listen to the doctors / tell your family / listen to the doctors / start bleeding at fifteen / listen to the doctors / change to weekly appointments / listen to the doctors / then get admitted / listen to the doctors / after your sonogram / listen to the doctors / stare at ultrasound strips / listen to the doctors / trace the block print / listen to the doctors / *it's a girl!* / listen to the doctors / get in bed / listen to the doctors / *try not to stress* / listen to the doctors / *move as little as you can* / listen to the doctors / *we need more tests* / listen to the doctors / pee in this bucket / listen to the doctors / wake up to needle-tips / listen to the doctors / thermometer communion / listen to the doctors / too many gloved hands / listen to the doctors / rubber fingerprints / listen to the doctors / be touched by everyone / listen to the doctors / when you want to be touched by no one / listen to the doctors / lose yourself in mantra / listen to the doctors / as speculums split you open / listen to the doctors / *it's for the baby* / listen to the doctors / *for the baby, you can do this* / listen to the doctors / let them touch you / listen to the doctors / *you can do this* / listen to the doctors / stare at the doorway / listen to the doctors / to the room of lost sons / listen to the doctors / *you're crying too much* / listen to the doctors / beg to go home / listen to the doctors / *biweekly appointments* / listen to the doctors / find your regular specialist / listen to the doctors / is on vacation / listen to the doctors / when the snow-capped stranger / listen to the doctors / shows up instead of her / listen to the doctor / reads your swollen file / listen to the doctor / as you wait in stirrups / listen to the doctor / from between your bent knees / listen to the doctor / *it's for the baby* / listen to the doctor / don't worry about the blood / listen to the doctor / *DNA test is back* / listen to the doctor / *oh, look at that* / listen to the doctor / *you're rare and interesting* / listen to the doctor / *compound heterozygous* / listen to the doctor / *on a blood-clotting gene* / listen to the doctor / *that doesn't sound good* / listen to the doctor / he squeezes your socked foot / listen to the doctor / instead of kicking him / listen to the doctor / *you can do this* / listen to the doctor / *does this mean you can save her?* / listen to the doctor / shuffle papers / listen to the doctor / *well, honey* / listen to the doctor / *it's for the*

IT'S HARD TO THINK ABOUT ANYTHING BUT TO BREATHE

Weary—that's how you appear, caught in memory, the moment before you
Hear me shiver, shift beneath the ER's crepe-thin, paper blanket. Instantly,
   an
Encouraging smile blossoms; your spine straightens like a daffodil piercing
   spring
Numb to winter's chill, the clockwork screams, this morning's blood-stained
   sheets.

Under your green gaze, apologies die on my lips; my body, that traitor who
   just

Let a second child slip into the riptide of grief, awaits its trial, beached here
On the rickety gurney, ready for blame, not this tenderness that suddenly
   fades the I-
V's pinch across my wrist—frigid press of the ultrasound eased, technician
   hunting
Errant remnants forgotten as I sink into your watery stare, tread there.
   Breathe. In

Sports team tee and jeans, you sit, dimly lit in the distance, and I think, *There*
   is no
Other man for me. No words seem necessary—the anchor of you across the
   hospital room
Means we'll be okay, even with bough breached by another forever pain, that
   never-
Ending loss of our son, now doubled with a daughter. We don't know the
   flood has just
Begun, two loved fathers to follow. To keep afloat, we bottle up syllables, set
   corked pleas

Out to sea, adrift in glass; whispers trapped in seashells keep our secret aches, images of

Dreams where our babies breathe and your dad, that romantic, appears too late to

Yell us ashore—our tongues bitten, marriage drowned in a mouthful of blood.

THE LONG GOODNIGHT
for Diana

Dad wakes up, has forgotten where he is, what's happened.
A daughter on each side of the slim, white bed, telling why
he can't rip the IV needle out, relieve its throbbing pinch.
We hold his hands, remind him, he's in hospital, has fallen.

A daughter on each side of the slim, white bed, telling why
but he doesn't understand, has become a toddler again, so
we hold his hands, remind him, he's in hospital, has fallen
try to pry him from Alzheimer's grip, explain it to him

but he doesn't understand, has become a toddler again, so
each time he drifts back from his sea of sleep, we restart
try to pry him from Alzheimer's grip, explain it to him.
Please, we know it hurts, but the doctor says you need it.

Each time he drifts back from his sea of sleep, we restart—
he can't rip the IV needle out, relieve its throbbing pinch.
Please, we know it hurts, but the doctor says you need it.
Dad wakes up, has forgotten where he is, what's happened.

ANOTHER ART

The art of Alzheimer's is hard to master;
first, the forgetting seems simple, but then
the doctor's diagnosis—it's disaster.

You curse hours lost, searching over and over
for things just held—glasses, keys, book, pen.
The art of Alzheimer's is hard to master.

Forget what you love: golf, cars, computers—
fade in a prescribed haze of medicines.
Swallow pills with hope you'll avert disaster.

Cry through Friday lunches when you remember
working, driving, the man you'd been when
Alzheimer's wasn't yet your art to master.

Then lose those memories, tears, words and numbers
names and dates; your own birthday now forgotten
in sick magician's trick, approaching disaster.

Four days of coma dreams, courting the hereafter
and then your brain forgets to breathe again.
The art of Alzheimer's, a killing master—
so many deaths precede that last disaster.

POEM IN WHICH DAD LIVES PAST SIXTY-SEVEN

In this poem, Alzheimer's doesn't steal my father's mind five years before it takes his life, so today I'll head to his and Susan's place, peruse his assortment of creamers as he brews us a fresh pot of dark roast, follow his trail of Old Spice onto the patio, where Susan's continued cigarette smoking doesn't worry us one bit because cancer can't penetrate these lines either. Here, Dad gets back more than the decade we've lost so far: seventy-seven and still a scratch golfer, he meets all three of his grandkids instead of just one, fills their cartoon-covered bellies weekly with ice cream, reads, reads, reads, then finally writes that sci-fi novel. In this poem, he gets our wish, opposite of his father's, to keep our brains while these bodies, stale cookies, crumb away. Here, some tiny peach pill taken twice a day with meals dissolves those plaques between his neurons, like wall stains hit by a magic eraser, and returns him to me— spread ashes gathered from the sea.

WHEN I JOIN THE BORG COLLECTIVE

they will finally stop—all these feelings, piled up like drone parts, nanoprobes to grow my replacement heart, the metal kind, this time impenetrable. I wait—mind stilled, a smoked bee. No more poems will be necessary. No need to make sense of dandelion seeds, poets shot on Myanmar streets. The hive will assimilate it all—no need for speech—while the queen, collector of sorrows, scatters the bits of me, flips the m upside down, turns me to we finally and finally.

ANNIVERSARY PANTOUM

February arrives again, robs me of sense.
Fetus memories fill the empty vase of me.
No flowers, please—there's enough dying already.
The petals fall. I watch on, numb as a bee sting as

fetus memories fill the empty vase of me.
I send Valentines to ghosts, loves lost.
The petals fall. I watch on, numb as a bee sting, as
a burn in between first sear and pulse throb.

I send Valentines to ghosts, loves lost,
hunt reasons why death took my son, left me
a burn in between first sear and pulse throb.
Lightning strike bad luck, the doctors said. *Try again.*

Hunt reasons why death took my son, left me
on bedrest, the next petal's fall in slow motion.
Lightning strike bad luck, the doctors said. *Try again.*
I've survived this ward before, know what happens

on bedrest, the next petal's fall in slow motion.
No flowers, please—there's enough dying already.
I've survived this ward before, know what happens.
February arrives again, robs me of sense.

THE CURSE OF THE DOG, THE SUNFLOWER AND THE YOUNG MOTHER

To be cursed
complained the dog
is to have your mom
home
all day
but not allowed
to move or play

To be cursed
complained the sunflower
is to sit on the sill
brightness
ignored except when
your petals fell

To be cursed
complained the young mother
is to love unsprung seeds
so hard
while you watch them
wash right through you
like broken water

HAVING MY SPONTANEOUS ABORTION MANSPLAINED AS A MISCARRIAGE, OR, TO THE COLLEAGUE WHO SAID, *IT'S PROBABLY FOR THE BEST*

You could have just filleted me there
on the mailroom floor instead

then I wouldn't need to show up
for Comp. I class, grief refastened

a worn-in red cardigan
buttoned up so high it chokes

the failure looped around my neck
like a latchkey to a burned-down house

and my throat was already full of bones
shorn feathers of hope

so it was probably
for the best

that I said nothing
but the vacant stare

syllables of the *Fuck off* thought stuck
in the amber-thick depression

repooling at my feet
like memories of broken water

and ruined things
I swore I'd left back home

next to the newborn-sized clothes
Christmas gifts waiting

for the child who arrived
too early

too still
still lungless

as the stand of trees
green canvas I watched for a week

willing the wind to resuscitate their branches
let me see them breathe.

CLOCK

n. A machine of great moral value to man, allaying his concern for the future by reminding him what a lot of time remains to him.

—Ambrose Bierce

Hung first in memory on elementary school walls
circular, black and white god, master of bells

I command subjects, turn math to English, history
to lunch, govern teachers and students alike in

my slow crawl through middle and high school
periods. I answer the morning's first question

am the last concern at night. You set me
then upset me with daily, flailing strikes

snooze through thirty years of careers
where you first learn I can be a verb—

each quarter hour turned to quarters, then
dollars—then retirement and too little time

for the part-time Edwin Watts job, favorite
pastimes, before Alzheimer's seals its fist

turns me to a bracelet on your wrist.

BEDREST AT WINNIE PALMER

In this poem, it wasn't all for nothing: weeks of bedside peeing in white construction buckets in view of the room where we lost our son; the social worker, suited siren waving from the shores of sanity, worried I'm crying too much; the stuttered crawl of the wall clock's second hand, ticking off another minute I've kept our daughter safe, kept her inside, kept her—this time, long enough.

REFLECTION

n. An action of the mind whereby we obtain a clearer view of our relation to the things of yesterday and are able to avoid the perils that we shall not again encounter.

—Ambrose Bierce

I feel her still, thirty-five-year-old
me, desperate as a dying wish

on the twin-sized bed, told a moment
standing upright could mean her child's

downfall, so she waits like bitter
fruit for the ripening.

Hospital gown knots, a string of peas
run down her spine, steal her sleep.

For half a moon, she watches clock hands
spin, shower-capped nurses changing shifts

pouring liquids into lined cups, then
noting the ounces peed into bedside

buckets, measuring to see if and when
her water will break again, trigger

another avalanche of grief
when no amount of unmoving

can save this second baby.

EMPTY NEST

You remember the children you got that you did not get . . .
—Gwendolyn Brooks

That first morning after is the worst—you
instinctively reach for her only to remember
you've failed once again, are as empty as the
abandoned house across the street, children
falling through the faulty floorboards you
call a body. Train-engine heartbeat you got
to hear each week at the doctor's office, that
jelly-bean body, the flurry of feet that you
watched on the black & white screen but did
not ever get to see in color, this daughter not
to be met—ultrasound memories, all we get.

WHEN THE ORDERLY WHEELS ME OUT AFTERWARD

there is a family
loading up their SUV

fumbling with the baby seat
as the morning sun winks

off shiny Mylar balloons
blinding pink hues of confetti

exploding around the words:
Congratulations! It's a girl!

and I can't swallow
the hiccupped sob

before the new mother hears
turns—smile caught

on my balloonless chair
puffer fish eyelids, watery stare

no cart of bouquets behind
to pack in the backseat

no baby
just this lapful of grief

just me, watching the family
I thought we would be

as I wait for my husband
to pull up, rescue me.

RECIPE FOR MARITAL DISASTER

Level: Easy   Total Time: 11 years   Active: 5 Years   Yield: 1 Divorce

Ingredients:

2 babies lost at 21 weeks
1 father with early-onset Alzheimer's
1 father at 90, bedridden in living room hospital bed
1 14-year-old witness
2 depressed spouses
23.5 daily hours of silence between them
0 meaningful topics addressed
0 snuggling
0 sex

Directions: Fuck if I know—it all just happened while we tried to take care of our dads, the 14-year-old, stay afloat.

Test Kitchen Tip: Once started, you might not be able to quit making this.

Facts (per serving)

291g sorrow   47g loneliness   12g regret

WHAT WILL I THINK OF MY TATTOOS

if, like Dad, my mind is lost
to Alzheimer's too?

Will Angel Bunny with her heart-
dotted fruits transport me

to toddler Meg running through
1999's Elmo sprinkler

in her Sesame Street, *Cherries
are cheery!* two piece?

Or perhaps I'll believe it's Big
Bunny, the rather small stuffed

rabbit from that first Easter
basket back in '73, the '70s

which could now feel more real
more memorable than the menu

of my last meal, which I worry
might have meat, if the disease

makes me discard half a life-
time of vegetarianism

like some sick magic trick played
by the tulip-topped Luna

wand on my left arm. Perhaps
I'll even forget the feathered

hope of poetry, wonder
at the quill inked onto me

but I'm sure to know the dark
birds etched over my heart

remember lost babies.

NUTRITION PROBLEMS

She slices apples for lunch in happy return, at least, to vegetarianism. Packs almonds, granola bar, flip phone, and gradebook. Fixes coffee to make possible two morning meetings of Comp. I. Grabs the keys, a spare umbrella from the hall closet. Unpacks her heart from the top shelf's hatbox. Swallows it down with a gulp of mocha. Wishes she hadn't. Especially when, remembering the school's overactive a/c, she needs to head back to the bedroom for a cardigan. Passes the new room, the newest wound, the would-be nursery, now never to be used beyond spouse's closet/storage room for dirty laundry. Beside its shut white door, she's stuck in towering stacks of onesies tucked in mint green dresser drawers, the plush ladybug wall art, next year's Goodwill donation, gathering dust on the bedroom floor.

Quiz on this section:

a. How does your reading of the passage change if the pronouns are switched from *she* to *he . . . you . . . they*?
b. How much more meat (round to the nearest pound, please) would the main character have needed to eat to save the baby?
c. During the year lease, how many times did the protagonist pass the never-to-be nursery? (Closest guess wins a spare copy of *What to Expect When You're Expecting*, which has sections on being pregnant while "Vegetarian" and "Red-Meat-Free.")
d. Were those ladybugs ever hung on a living child's wall? If so, attach the room's diagram (preferably hand-drawn).

UNDERWATER

She hides outside this white-walled room
the never-painted nursery

grief pulling at her hems
like a toddler.

She sits, swaddles it
long enough for her funeral blacks

to ivy over. Unfinished flowers
fall from her skirts. Red petals.

Motherhood, the bright bulb
her moth-heart circles

though she knows
it might kill her.

Family, her mermaid's dream of legs
of underwater Ferris Wheels

spinning possibilities, turned
sick circle, sad carnival of ovaries.

She wakes, another day to choke
down her ocean of loss

the pecking thoughts:
Was it because, because, because . . . ?

HEADED HOME AGAIN

Submarine, scene of fear's first memory: blue-uniformed Dad
Leans over the open hatch, smiles, passes toddler-me downward
Into some strange sailor's arms. A throat-knot steals my scream.
Panic shoots through preschool limbs too soon without him, fingers

Stretching for his face in the circle of sky above. The shock of being
Let go does not wear off. It's thirty-odd years into the future, three
Into Alzheimer's lost ocean of thoughts. We spend Fridays together,
Dining out and talking to folks, two of his last pleasures. At the cafe
I watch him offer handshakes to the baseball-capped veterans, wave at
Nearby kids peeking over booth-tops, order his usual (scrambled eggs
'n bacon, wheat toast, a chocolate muffin wrapped to-go), pointing at

An upside-down menu, pretending to read the words. The knot returns,
Wedges in my throat. I sense the hole opening below our checkered table
And feel his mind letting go, dementia rushing me into the arms of the
Years ahead—close to a decade now of searching skyward for him.

The Marriage Question

Envision us now   two bodies
two paths   moving and
choosing our   own courses
So idiotic   thinking
two celestial-   bodied
selves   could
                                              collide
                                              form
                                              some
                                              greater
                                              republic
                                          a newer
                                          perfect
                                        planet
                                      marriage
                                    No, we
                                  still plot
                              our orbits
                          parallel or
                        juxtaposed
                    hedge the
                  ecliptic
              moments
            when the
          gravity
        of one
      pulls
    too close
  threatens
to end this
planetary
dance

          Each
          day we
        choose be-
      cause no one
    truly knows how
      love happens
        or how it
          should
            go

GETTING READY

for Anna Mae

We dress for mass:
my white tights   her sheer stockings
my lacy slip   her elastic girdle
and I wonder why she still wears a girdle.
Grandpa's dead. Who's she got to impress?
It's for God, she says.

We walk down the aisle
pick our pew and genuflect.
I'm plotting the timeline of my life:
two years   ears pierced
three   those sheer stockings
four   my first date
beyond that   the girdle I guess
a man's unfinished face
small mouths, loud cries
then he will die
and I will dress for God.

ALL AROUND YOUR ISLAND, THERE'S A BARRICADE

When the winter moon
Arrives with its tidal pull
Lift your chill-dotted
Limbs back into the stirrups—
Splayed creature caught, the tide's fool.

Wake to crimson shock
Again, another morning
Linens soaked with loss
Lake of blood, pool of mourning
Spots that will never wash off.

Water broken like
All your dreams of family.
List of those to phone
Leers from the desktop—top names
Slashed through dreams of family.

When Alzheimer's rips
Away your careful walls, you'll
Live over the loss—
Labor first, the bathroom birth
Son saved, jarred for the doctors.

PLEASE STOP CALLING THIS SPONTANEOUS ABORTION

What the doctors call
spontaneous abortion—
forty mornings of
linens stained red, your child dead
no matter your intentions.

WHAT LOSING A BABY AT TWENTY-ONE WEEKS DOESN'T FEEL LIKE, AN ERASURE

spontaneous

natural   free
voluntary   of one's own accord
graceful

unconstrained

instinctive

a natural process
external   self-contained

without
labour   coming into
existence

WHEN THE THERAPIST ASKS IF I CAN STOP GRIEVING BABIES LOST TEN YEARS AGO

this time I agree to pack them up—the palm-sized son the pink-capped nurses dressed in tiny train pajamas, delivered in a wicker basket, perfect except for the stillness, which I'll tuck next to the empty visage of his sister, whisked away and cut before I could, so I never would, see her in anything but these thin strips of already fading prints, ultrasound Rorschachs I let fall in this box of loss beside February dreams in which my children breathe and I live.

THE CRUELEST MONTH

isn't April—
at least for me
the wasteland comes
in the last month
the Romans made
with its unluckily even
twenty-eight days.
No burials here
no lilacs sprung
from the dead—
their two
too tiny bodies
taken for tests
then incinerated
as I wish
this grief
could be
but instead
it seeps
like February
sometimes does
beyond its
usual borders.

A LITTLE PREPOSITION

*April 21—Mrs. Agnes Thompson Kelley, wife of John Kelley, the well-known
manufacturer of rustic work, died of childbirth Saturday morning.*

—*The Daily Morning Journal and Courier*
(New Haven, CT), April 22, 1895

Today I got stuck in a phrase
from my great-great-grandmother's
obituary—there it was
in graying print
what my Gram and I suspected
but never could confirm
that her mother's mother, too
had *died of childbirth.*

Childbirth, happy noun
turned by the power
of that little preposition—
that *of, of, of*
squawking off the page
for notice like a newborn—
into a cause of death
like stroke or cancer.

Childbirth, the same term
in her time for success
in the endeavor
and its opposite—
that awful *of*
replaced for us now
by the more innocent *in.*

A SECOND TO CHANGE

Work clothes folded neatly
on the exam room seat

bra and panties tucked
safely between layers

of black pencil skirt and
red button-up sweater

I stand naked
except for the socks

I've learned to pack
to protect chill-prone feet

from the stirrups'
unforgiving metal.

I reach for the papery gown
unfold its coarse, pink fabric—

opposite of the blue, over-washed
ones worn at the hospital—

the creped texture, a relief
as it grazes against my skin

and I attempt to unravel
the riddle of closure.

THE SPACE I WILL NEED FOR MY BAGGAGE

FEBRUARY FORECAST

I am a cathedral of deadbolts / and I'd rather burn myself down / than change the locks.
—Rachel McKibbens

The stream of January days dwindling means I
am about to fall. Storm-whipped branch, I am
roof litter, unwanted chore, annual cleanup, a
house of bleeding doors, an abandoned cathedral
turned club. Midnight black light flashes off of
stained glass stations of the cross. Deadbolts
don't grow on hearts but can be fashioned and
installed—quick, before the memory flood. I'd
miss them more or less, do you think, if rather
than pack it all into one month, my mind burn-
ed the sky black all year long? A pyre. Myself
as kindling. Or mulch. Let the worms slide down
my arteries, find chambers of a heart larger than
could be borne. Shadows of loss stretch, change
with each winter harvest of ungrown seeds, the
woman surviving here by sliding home her locks.

HOW A MONTH BECOMES A TIDAL FORCE

February floods like broken water in our bed—rafts of sad blood between us for so long we do not notice. It surges like a father's dream of holding a grandchild washed downstream. It overruns like the plaques in the other dad's head, missives slipping into riptide, personality pulled to sea. It overflows with breakthrough memories, iceberg tips sharp as my own clipped voice still willing the impossible, asking the nurse one last time, *Is he breathing?* It engulfs. Each winter now, a tidal pool of grief, pulling at the jagged shorelines of me. It floods like a namesake plain, like a namesake, but still, there is no thawing me.

EVEN AFTER FIFTEEN YEARS

this shortest month slices to bone
like your first apartment's window pane
the one through which your forearm flew
when you fought its paint-stuck frame.

Now grief's white glue binds your brokenness
seals things, like your moth-heart, shut.
Plucked hopes stacked on the cutting board
keep singed wings away from further flame

from that siren song of motherhood
finishing always in funeral dirge
in two February deathdays
you write to endure.

VALENTINES YOU SEND WHEN YOU'VE LOST BABIES ON FEBRUARY 10TH AND 21ST

1. Love Letter to the Birth Month That Should Have Been

July, you do not burn me
like February does

with its birthdays being
deathdays all at once.

No, you sit safely
at the center of the year

an unwrapped present
unlit firework

month when their lives
could have begun

if only I/they
could have held on.

2. Hate Mail to the Birth Month That Was

February, your winter gloom
twisted in Florida's
perpetual green

still manages to unearth
memories of white sheets
a clean blanket of snow

pooling red—where
does she begin
do I end

will this ever end
end happily
will I ever see

Valentines
and not think
of lost things?

LOST PANTOUM

Now you can't find your sentences.
Are they hidden in the ice box
where once we looked for treasures:
your keys, remote, glasses, watch?

Are they hidden in the ice box
forgotten on the office desk like
your keys, remote, glasses, watch?
Will we ever finish unearthing things

forgotten on the office desk like
that legal pad, the novel you began?
Will we ever finish unearthing things—
syllables strewn, verbs tossed?

That legal pad, the novel you began
slipping into Alzheimer's grip—
syllables strewn, verbs tossed
just ghost notes, punctuated loss.

Slipping into Alzheimer's grip
now you can't find your sentences—
just ghost notes, punctuated loss
where once we looked for treasures.

PRAY

v. To ask that the laws of the universe be annulled in behalf of a single petitioner confessedly unworthy.

—Ambrose Bierce

On this day of little angels
I've lost you once again—

no point in spreading marigolds
bright flowers for the dead.

To call your souls would be unfair
with nothing real to offer

no favorite toys
no foods to share

no photos for your altars—
just this mother who knows

nothing but the syllables
of your names

how hard she prayed
to save you

that you both
died anyway.

THE TAROT OF LETTING GO

I gave away the copy of *War and Peace*
begun on bedrest, attempting to save

Anna, new babe named for the already
lost, like any hope of finishing

either pregnancy or novel
sight of the bright blue cover

enough to make the world blur
so I gave it up

marriage, house, book
kept as few reminders

as possible. The sonogram strips
continue to fade like the woman

I was—wife, mother, daughter—
nothing stuck, nothing but me

in this tar pool of grief
blindfolded, surrounded

by a garden of sword-stalks.

NOT A CINDERELLA STORY

I don't need reminders.
I still live
in your neighborhood
pick up groceries
at your Publix
push my cart past
coffee-creamer-corner
where you stood
countless times—
your personal mission
to find
to taste
every new variety.

I don't need e-mail reminders
around all holidays
from vendors
wanting to send you presents.
I already know
a Mimi's gift card
would have been
the perfect gift—
corn chowder
dashed with pepper to begin
eggs, scrambled
bacon, crisp
washed down with orange juice
the chocolate muffin wrapped to go—
five years of Fridays.

I don't need reminders.
The Barnes and Noble mailer
must be a joke—
the latest western, spy, and sci-fi
you couldn't have read
in the end
when Alzheimer's
stole all
of the words
years before
it stole you.

I don't need the giant sign,
"Don't forget Dad—June 16th."
The rows of man-colored cards
blue envelopes I'll never label
tumble over me, tumble me over.
I got the call yesterday:
you're at sea finally
and finally.

I don't need a reminder
that life is not a fairytale
that no sparkly dress will fix this
certainly not shoes
when what I want—
you back
and whole—
is as impossible
as a bird
dropping wishes
fruit for the unspoiled

from a tear-grown tree
but if that is you
smiling down from heaven
in the seam of a cloud
the surrounding sky
the same blue of your eyes—
that reminder
I'll take it.

MY DAD ADORED COFFEE

and if he loved you too
he'd make you a cup
brewed whichever way
his latest research
and gadgetry
prescribed best—
drip
press
some new bean
darker roast
finer grind
better yet
bounce in his step
he'd dash beyond
the kitchen island
open the fridge door
like a prize show model
revealing not some new car
but a top shelf
crammed with creamers
shiny new hybrids
of fruits and spices
lined up
for your selection—
everything then
at your fingertips
like the steaming mug
he hands you
and only now
do you begin
to understand it.

HAIBUN FOR THE OPEN ROAD

In February, the few Florida trees that will lose their leaves have begun to turn—thankfully, no more shocks of red, just mocking greens, punctuated by the occasional patch of yellow Live Oaks.

Staring out the windshield, I wish for a proper winter, empty womb of a world, peppered with bare branches. The thrumming breeze from the cracked passenger window whistles through the Jetta cabin as the expressway arches over the gray grid of Orlando's suburban streets. Notes of Sumatra and cocoa ribbon up from the beige cupholder's still-steaming mocha, a missed treat, exchanged for five months of orange juice and vitamins.

The cross-top of the First Baptist Church bobs its head over the horizon. Two minutes from home with its useless stack of infant hats, the aquamarine pack of Pampers. *Can we just keep driving?*

next February
cloud banks tuck in a full moon
the kindest darkness

ACKNOWLEDGMENTS & NOTES

805 Lit + Art: "How a Month Becomes a Tidal Force"

Atlas and Alice: "Underwater"

Bacopa Literary Review: "In the Last Year of Our Marriage" and "Please Stop Calling This Spontaneous Abortion"

Coffee People (Issues 16 & 19): "Haibun for the Open Road" and "My Dad Adored Coffee"

Delmarva Review: "Anniversary Pantoum"

DMQ Review: "Bedrest at Winnie Palmer," "When the Therapist Asks If I Can Stop Grieving Babies Lost Ten Years Ago," and "When I Join the Borg Collective"

Drunk Monkeys: "Clock"

Eclectica Magazine: "Each Time I Pull into Mom's Parking Spot"

The Fox Hat Review: "Another Art" and "Not a Cinderella Story"

Free State Review: "Reflection"

Funicular Magazine: "Poem in Which Dad Lives Past Sixty-Seven"

The Good Life Review: "Aftermath"

Hawai'i Pacific Review: "The Curse of the Dog, the Sunflower and the Young Mother"

Hole In The Head Review: "How to Get the Guy Between Your Legs to Say *You're Rare and Interesting*" and "Triptych to Wreck Diving"

I-70 Review: "Mourning Song"

Ibbetson Street Press: "Why, like the Tide, He Could Not Stop"

The Lake: "The Gender Reveal: A Quiz" and "Parenting Lessons"

LEON Literary Review: "Having My Spontaneous Abortion Mansplained as a Miscarriage, or, To the Colleague Who Said, *It's Probably for the Best*"

Lips Poetry Magazine: "A Second to Change"

long con magazine: "It's Hard to Think About Anything but to Breathe"

Molecule: a tiny lit mag: "The Space I Will Need for My Baggage"

MQR Mixtape: "Recipe for Marital Disaster"

New Ohio Review: "On Our Way Home"

NonBinary Review: "Getting Ready"

The Orchards Poetry Journal: "February Forecast"

Pangyrus: "Nutrition Problems"

Please See Me (Issues 3 & 10): "Empty Nest," "This Is the Floor Where No Babies Are Saved," "Waiting Room Blues," and "When the Orderly Wheels Me out Afterward"

Prospectus: "Not Again" and "Planning My Escape"

Proud to Be: Writing by American Warriors, Volume 11 (Southeast Missouri State UP): "Headed Home Again"

Slant: "The Tarot of Letting Go"

South Florida Poetry Journal: "Pray"

SWWIM Every Day: "Lost Pantoum"

Tipton Poetry Journal: "The Long Goodnight"

untethered: "The Marriage Question"

Yellow Arrow Journal: "The Cruelest Month"

"Aftermath" and "Nutrition Problems" are after the poems in *Story Problems* by Charles Jenson.

"Mourning Song" is after "Morning Song" by Sylvia Plath.

"Tired of Fighting" responds to "Lost Cause" by Beck.

"Not Again" and "Poem in Which Dad Lives Past Sixty-Seven" are after "A Poem in Which No Black People Are Dead" by Hanif Abdurraqib.

"Triptych to Wreck Diving" contains a quote as an epigraph from "Diving into the Wreck" by Adrienne Rich.

"Believing Every Word They Said Was True" responds to "Fool for Love" by Sandy Rogers.

"Have to Have Poison Skin" responds to "Stay Away" by Nirvana and is after "The night, the street, street-lamp, drugstore . . ." by Aleksandr Blok, translated by Vladimir Markov and Merrill Sparks.

"Planning My Escape" responds to "Spiderwebs" by No Doubt.

"It's Hard to Think About Anything but to Breathe" responds to "When U Love Somebody" by Fruit Bats.

"Another Art" is after "One Art" by Elizabeth Bishop.

"The Curse of the Dog, the Sunflower, and the Young Mother" is after "The Blessing of the Old Woman, the Tulip, and the Dog" by Alicia Ostriker.

"Clock," "Reflection," and "Pray" respond to definitions from *The Devil's Dictionary* by Ambrose Bierce.

"Empty Nest" is a golden shovel after "the mother" by Gwendolyn Brooks.

"Underwater" responds to "El Camino de Esmeralda" by Danelle Rivas, the *Rattle* Ekphrastic Challenge image for May 2022.

"Headed Home Again" responds to "Slip Slidin' Away" by Paul Simon.

"All Around Your Island, There's a Barricade" responds to "Walls (Circus)" by Tom Petty & the Heartbreakers.

"What Losing a Baby at Twenty-One Weeks Doesn't Feel Like, an Erasure" is an erasure of the definition of "spontaneous" from *The Shorter Oxford English Dictionary,* vol. 2, Oxford UP, 2002.

"The Cruelest Month" is after "The Waste Land" by T. S. Eliot.

"A Second to Change" responds to "Anonymous Was a Woman" by Natascha Graham, the *Rattle* Ekphrastic Challenge image for March 2022.

"February Forecast" is a golden shovel after "Letter from My Heart to My Brain" by Rachel McKibbens.

THANKS

"A literary work is a communal act. And this book could not have been imagined, let alone conceived, without the help of many people," writes Michael Ondaatje in *Running in the Family*, and I feel similarly blessed. Thanks first to the brilliant and generous Eugenia Leigh, whose teaching and advice were integral during the revision of this manuscript, and to the fierce and fabulous Courtney LeBlanc at Riot in Your Throat, for believing in this collection and bringing it to life in its best possible form.

Thanks also to the wonderful humans with whom these poems were created and/or workshopped: my creative writing students and colleagues at Valencia College (shout outs of love for Diane Orsini and Jackie Zuromski for two decades of support and inspiration), my wizard-art family—especially Claudia Morales, Danielle Gennaro, and Olivia Dolphin—and poet friends and instructors from the Brooklyn Poets, *Chestnut Review* and Hudson Valley Writers Center, communities whose insights, prompts and feedback helped shape this work, with special thanks to Joan Kwon Glass, Rosebud Ben-Oni, James Rawlings, Shilo Niziolek, and Eileen Oldag.

Thank you to the amazing professors at the University of Central Florida who nurtured my love of literature and writing, especially Judith Hemschemeyer, Jocelyn Bartkevicius, Lisa Logan, Pat Rushin, and Jeanne Leiby. Thanks as well to Valencia College for granting sabbatical leave in the fall semester of 2022, which made the initial drafts of this manuscript possible.

Unending gratitude to family and friends whose support through the happy highs and, of course, repeated rejections along this poetry journey has been invaluable, with extra love and thanks to the most wonderful sister, Diana Mainieri, and amazing kid and fellow-poet, Megan Markham. Finally, special thanks to Neil Sebacher, and the greatest gift of a best friend, Bridgette Megharief, whose love and care kept me afloat through the years captured in these poems.

ABOUT THE AUTHOR

Jill Michelle is the author of the chapbook *Shuffle Play* (Bottlecap Press, 2024) and winner of the 2023 NORward Prize for Poetry. Her poems have appeared in *DMQ Review, Drunk Monkeys, New Ohio Review, Rust & Moth, SWWIM Every Day,* and other publications. She received her MA from the University of Central Florida and, since 2000, has taught writing and literature at Valencia College in Orlando, Florida. Her favorite things are music, sci-fi, soccer and her sweet Boston Terrier, Whimsy. Find more at byjillmichelle.com and on Bluesky and IG: @jillpoppyflower.

ABOUT THE PRESS

Riot in Your Throat is an independent press that
publishes fierce, feminist poetry.

Support independent authors, artists, and presses.

Visit us online:
www.riotinyourthroat.com

RIOT IN YOUR THROAT BOOKS

www.ingramcontent.com/pod-product-compliance
Lightning Source LLC
Chambersburg PA
CBHW020800130626
46554CB00006B/2279